my first book of

NUMBERS

1

One

2

Two

3

Three

4

Four

5

Five

6

Six

7

Seven

8

Eight

9

Nine

10

Ten

11

Eleven

12

Twelve

13

Thirteen

14

Fourteen

15

Fifteen

16

Sixteen

17

Seventeen

18

Eighteen

19

Nineteen

20

Twenty

Time to Revise!

1	2	3
4	5	6
7	8	9
	10	

11 12 13

14 15 16

17 18 19

20

my first book of
NUMBERS

This board book has been specially designed to keep your baby engaged and away from harmful TV/mobile screens. Keeping in mind your baby's attention span and learning needs, this book will help in:

1) Improving your baby's observation skills.
2) Helping your baby identify basic numbers.
3) Enhancing your baby's vocabulary.

Also available as an **e-book**

Children

ISBN 978-93-5520-591-9

9 789355 205919

MOONSTONE

www.rupapublications.co.in